Looking for Light

Looking for Light

Susan Ioannou

First Edition

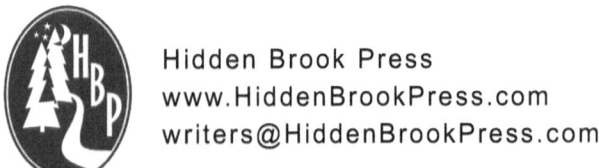

Hidden Brook Press
www.HiddenBrookPress.com
writers@HiddenBrookPress.com

Copyright © 2016 Hidden Brook Press
Copyright © 2016 Susan Ioannou

All rights for poems revert to the author. All rights for book, layout and design remain with Hidden Brook Press. No part of this book may be reproduced except by a reviewer who may quote brief passages in a review. The use of any part of this publication reproduced, transmitted in any form or by any means, electronic, mechanical, photocopied, recorded or otherwise stored in a retrieval system without prior written consent of the publisher is an infringement of the copyright law.

Looking for Light
by Susan Ioannou

Cover Image – Keith Wood
Cover Design – Richard M. Grove
Layout and Design – Richard M. Grove

Typeset in Garamond
Printed and bound in USA
Distributed: in USA by Ingram – 1-800-937-0152
          in Canada by Hidden Brook Distribution
          http://www.hiddenbrookpress.com/hidden-brook-distribution/

Library and Archives Canada Cataloguing in Publication

Ioannou, Susan, 1944-, author
     Looking for light / Susan Ioannou. -- 1st edition.

Poems.
ISBN 978-1-927725-34-4 (paperback)

    I. Title.

PS8567.O263L65 2016   C811'.54   C2016-901568-8

For my family

Acknowledgments

Some of the poems in this collection have been published in the following journals and anthologies: *Arc/Cordite Poetry Review, Ars Medica, A Tapestry in Six Textures, A Time of Trial, Canadian Author, Desperately Seeking Susans, Kavyam* (translated into Hindi), *Lake: A Journal of Arts and Environment, Literary Network, Other Voices, paperplates, Potato Eyes, Rhubarb, Seeds, The Annex Echo, The Poet's Quest for God, Treeline, Vallum, Who Would Be a God?, Women's Education des femmes, [Word]*, and *Ygdrasil*.

Cover Image: *Misty Mountains*
by Keith Wood, Whisky Emporium/Dreamstime

Table of Contents

Acknowledgments – *p. 9*
Foreword – Chris Faiers – *p. 13*

PART 1 – *Make It Beautiful*

Make It Beautiful – *p. 15*
Bagni di Lucca – *p. 18*
Imagine That Greek Island – *p. 24*
Landlords – *p. 25*
Night Train Through Matapedia – *p. 26*
Entente – *p. 30*
Poetry Class – *p. 31*
A Modern Poet and His Muse – *p. 32*
The Artist Passes – *p. 34*
Latin Dancer – *p. 35*
Sculptor – *p. 36*
Pelican – *p. 38*
Jinn – *p. 40*

PART 2 – *Beyond Knowing*

Creator – *p. 43*
Looking – *p. 44*
Far North – *p. 45*
Who Would Be a God? – *p. 46*
In Search of New Credos – *p. 47*
At Midnight – *p. 49*
The Listeners – *p. 50*
Lake Sounds – *p. 51*
First Snow – *p. 52*
(In)Substantial – *p. 53*
Photon – *p. 54*
God Particle – *p. 55*
Scientist – *p. 56*
Spinning Top – *p. 57*
Quest – *p. 58*
Balance Sheet Dream – *p. 59*

PART 3 – *Passing Seventy*

Secret – *p. 61*
Bed – *p. 62*
Mini Stroke – *p. 63*
Stressed – *p. 64*
As the Days Grow Shorter – *p. 65*
Tightrope – *p. 66*
Eye Surgeon – *p. 67*
Tiny Bug in the Bathtub – *p. 68*
Rusting – *p. 69*
Weighing Ends – *p. 70*
Finale – *p. 71*
Passing – *p. 72*
Crossing – *p. 73*
Grieving – *p. 74*
Conversion – *p. 75*
Return – *p. 76*
Wishes – *p. 77*
Transparence – *p. 78*
Idea – *p. 79*

EPILOGUE
The Choice – *p. 81*

About the Author – *p. 82*

Foreword

I've known Susan Ioannou and her poetry for well over three decades. All, all the way back to our mutual friendship with the Cabbagetown Kid himself, Ted Plantos. Susan was the Associate Editor with Ted's mag, *Cross-Canada Writers' Quarterly* (later *Cross-Canada Writers' Magazine*). *WQ* was an important, seminal litmag, a people's poetry oriented mag, which contrasted with the stuffy hothouse mags produced by Canadian universities. The best, and possibly some of the worst, poets nationwide sent their poetry, screeds, dreams and letters to *WQ*—a creative experience I'd consider far more nourishing than a year or so spent in post grad writing classes, although Susan has taught a few of these along her literary path as well.

Susan has also taken the path few of her contemporaries have chosen. Susan chose a close relationship with her Muse, while others, often with lesser abilities, pursued whatever fleeting moments pass for fame in CanLit. She doesn't have a list of thirty or forty personal books weighing down her bookshelves; instead she's waited for her Muse to breathe slyly in her ear, and Susan has always listened attentively. In addition to publishing only her truly inspired poems, Susan did the unheard of, and published an almost equal number of books on the creative process, featuring many of her contemporaries as exemplars in these publications. I was honoured to be among the many to have had their poems chosen by Susan, and for this I'm ever grateful.

So to her collection. This is the summation of a poetry elder, who has now passed the milestone of seven decades, a time when the partyers, glad-handers and professional academics have left the stage, and the Muse's soft whisperings are but a forgotten memory. There is more true poetry, more beauty, knowledge and song—direct transmissions from Susan's Muse—in each of the three sections of this collection than in 99% of the entire typical Canuck poetry offering. Miss devouring this book, and you'll miss the heart, soul and wisdom of one of Canada's best and wisest poets.

Chris Faiers,
Poet, Publisher, Editor,
First recipient of the Milton Acorn People's Poetry Medal

PART 1
Make It Beautiful

Make It Beautiful

Make it beautiful,
whispered the Muse.

But how to ripple out syllables
as day by day foreign horizons
flame with metal and human flesh
streaming ever more hate and grief,
while even here, too many sleep
rag-piled on a sidewalk grate?

Beautiful?

Step into a stately old bank downtown.
What vision raised white stone to gleaming,
high-domed ceiling sculpted in rosettes and squares
where slender lamps' gold frosted panes
dangle serenely from wrought iron?
Calm echoes
footsteps and whispered delight,
so soothing, pale polished marble
counter-topped by a gold-plated rail
reflecting clients' debits and credits.
Spaciousness and good taste
soften hard commerce.

As if elegance in design
implies that money is good
like food in the belly and shelter,
and voices humming through silence
are better than in-screaming shells,
that trade brings plenty
more enduring than tanks,
and lucre need not be filthy
if carefully stewarded and shared.

Elsewhere, bold men
cascade through streets with banners,
or fortressed by bodyguards, pass laws.
The gentler load up crates of dressings and pills,
or oceans away, dig wells, rebuild a school,
and spoon out gruel and milk powder.
Can any "serve who only stand and wait"
by listening (or is it hiding?)
at the feet of the Muse?

A few blocks along, above street level
confronting a grand plaza of stone
backed by high glass and steel,
if a massive bronze charging bull
loomed from a grassy rectangle
would it be beautiful?

Scurrying passers-by
shrink between huge concrete planters'
profusion of crimsons, yellows, and pinks,
and dwarfed by monolithic towers,
few stop upon a stone bench to sun
or slow and turn around
to savour this uplifted expanse
—vast space contained
yet proffering release.

Such power interlocks I-beams
girding black curtain walls
that mirror each other
while high in blue, waft indifferent clouds.
Are monumental simplicity, mass,
vertical metaphors for ambition
rising steadier floor by floor
until from the penthouse
only a few gaze down?

But on the underside of the globe?
What must it take to face
another bleak dawn?
None thinks, in a refugee tent,
about fine mahogany dusted
or Bauhaus mirrors agleam.
Mammon craves sleek walls, high steel
set in geometry's pleasing spaces
to buffer the foreign news'
tallies of how many unknown
were overnight blown apart by hate
or fleeing by sea, drowned.

Make it beautiful?

If one does not march
or urge on committees
or ladle soup to a dirty hand in rags
(lacking the thick-enough skin
or nerve to take a stand)

is it enough only to peep
over the paper's edge and wonder
how to scribble words about beauty
despite some fanatic's fuse,
a child's swollen belly, or bullets?
What does it mean to honour the Muse?

Bagni di Lucca
For Merla McMurray and Harry Girling

I

"Shelley stayed there..."
The kindly professor smiled,
hearing your travel plans.
"Bagni di Lucca,
high in the wooded Tuscan hillsides
above the heat of the cities on the plains.

"With Mary and Claire
he made a *villeggiatura*,
renting from a Signor Chiappa
a small-gardened summer home,
its arbour of laurel trees
so thick the sun could not penetrate;
no sound, except the rushing Lima
through the valley below.

"Closing Ariosto and Plato,
morning and evening Shelley rode,
or strolled by the river
and up narrow paths
noisy with cicala, sweet-singing birds,
even a cuckoo,
crisscrossing the chestnut woods.

"Once, he climbed high as Prato Fiorito
and in the meadow's decaying sweetness
penned how violets, jonquils, and moss
'dart their arrowy odour through the brain
Till you might faint with that delicious pain.'

"At noon, hidden by alders
where water 'transparent as air'
spilled from steep rocks into pool below pool,
naked, he sat, cooling little by little,
reading Herodotus.

"Of the landscape, he wrote to a friend:
'I take great delight in watching
the changes in atmosphere here:
thundershowers break towards evening
to flocks of delicate clouds
or, growing, overshadow the moon.
Our fireflies are fading
but over and over, pale summer lightning
spreads across the night sky
and lights home the low-flying owl.'"

II

Reciting from Shelley,
white hair tilted back,
did the professor return
to Bagni di Lucca golden as dusk
melting the Tuscan hills,
or stroll toward sunlight, like Mary and Claire,
along the ramparts of Lucca's ninth-century stone?

Seventeen centuries,
those Ancient Roman streets frilled
outward to alleys and squares,
buttressed themselves in three walls,
and raising palace and church
fattened on trade in agriculture and silks.

Spreading up to the hills
sixteenth- and seventeenth-century villas
—Mansi, Torrigiani, Reale
(home of Elisa, Napoleon's sister)—
opened from frescoes, rococo facades
to shady parks, where fountains hid lovers
—even, perhaps, a youthful professor—
slipping among nymphea and grottoes.

III

Eighteen kilometres out of the way
skidding through high winds and rain,
you fix on the kindly professor back home
—the reason you rented this car
and promised three grumbling friends
a sylvan beauty like none they had seen.
Steeled, you grip the slippery wheel
and stare straight ahead through the sheeting panes.
On either side splatter by
smokestack, warehouse, factory, crane.

At last, you turn off the highway to find
from guidebook phrases long memorized
"the countryside dotted with villas",
and slithering down toward Devil's Bridge
face Shelley's once exquisite view
flooded—a valley oozing muck,
plastic bags, and shreds of paper
snaggled on branches and bushes.

IV

Below, approaching Lucca's bastioned walls
"undoubtedly one of Italy's most beautiful cities",
you squint through the windshield wipers
for one of four streaming gates to the saints
San Pietro, Donato, Paolino, or Santa Maria.
Where is the Via del Anfiteatro,
its "yellow mediaeval houses" looping "a green"?
—Nothing but narrow facades
whipped by the rain.

Park. Is it worth getting soaked
running to Duomo di San Martino,
"a masterpiece in the Pisan style",
for the "accurate portrait of Christ"
high on the wood crucifix
"carved in New Testament times by high-priest Nicodemus"?
What shivering Santa Croce procession
lights candles through the alleys tonight?

A few steps ahead of the car,
a café looks onto a lopsided square.
Inside, crowd steamy tourists and children.
Surely—you squeeze through, with a smile—
hot pasta, carafes of red wine
will soften the rain.
Your friends' three dripping faces glare:
You pay.

V

". . . a charming air, unscathed . . ."

Ascending mud hills, sodden dales, why glance back?
Shelley, your heart would burn.
But what of the kindly professor at home
awaiting night's fireflies?

Tell him, as eyes turn away,
"Yes, how lovely it *was*,
Shelley's Bagni di Lucca."

Imagine That Greek Island

Half bare on baked white rock
you'd overlook the bay.
The day is hot. Dry light
bronzes your skin
and water's turquoise
blinds, silvered with stars.

Over white stucco and red tiled roofs
a *taverna*'s *clarino* twists on the air.
Hear the shuffle of dancing
—*Kalamatianós, Hasápiko.*
Sniff the sweat and smoke
spitting as *souvlaki* turns.

In your hands
moist vine leaves, plucked
to roll with rice, ground meat,
lemon, and oil, are enough
for lean, rolled-shirtsleeved men
to swallow with *raki*
—their smiles
a foretaste of love
when the sun slips
its bloodied fin
under the wave.

Landlords

Crossing the gravel road,
two silk-sleeved city women,
wade thigh-high through the field.

Crickets' *chir-rip* and the wind rustling
long green slopes to mare's-tail clouds
are the only sounds beside their voices.

They stop for a moment, and look around:
that rural elusive peace
longed for, but never quite believed.

Reality squats down a rutted lane,
warped by rust, flat tires, a sagging roof.
Its tenants scrape toward winter:

>"Yeah, ma'am, we'll plough that ragweed under,
>scythe the ditch,
>clear auto parts off the lawn.

>"The rent?
>Yeah, well,
>y'see..."

On the smooth city women walk.
It's simple for them, just turn their backs
and find a warm boulder to sprawl on

where time and shadow drift into dreams,
and no shingles flap
against midnight rain.

Night Train Through Matapedia
Nation-dreaming

I

Beyond the rocking window, dusk
deepens from rose to velvet blue
as fading copses, fields race by
pulling across two solitudes
while the tracks *click-clack*
and sidings veer
off—behind
leaving a lone inverted V
where Saint-Hyacinthe disappears
behind the dream that rattles and sways
on into the night.

Mile after mile, the darkness thickens.
Ding-DING-ding, red flashes by.
Street lamps bleach an intersection.
Clustered houses dim and thin
to village outskirts, moonlit farms.
The land is heavy with shadows
except above, a prick of light
follows, forest by forest, field after field,
a quiet constant, pinning the night
over the shivering atmosphere.
The Evening Star, it must be,
first of a myriad needling through
to steady grey metal
rocking on, faster, nearer.

II

Slowing, the steel wheels spark and creak,
turning and grinding around
Lachine's rushing black water
toothpicked with shadow bridges over dark foam,
until whirlpools lengthen and calm
like oil sliding slow toward shore.
Far across, out of the darkness
green glows on a rising horizon,
Plains of Abraham phosphorescent
atop great Citadel cliffs
dropping to tiny glittering houses
and, blackening at the base,
the minuscule ovals of boats bobbing
—a midnight city, old and foreign,
so distant, yet magnificent, alone.
Separation: dark's oily rippling.
I wait and watch and wonder
how long. . . .

III

Tumble to the brink of the berth,
roll back into the wall,
how fast these wheels are thumping and squealing
upward and upward, straining
as if to hold on to rusted joints.

A few feet outside the blind,
dark is a cliff straight up
bristled steep with black pines
so high I cannot see their tips,
I cannot see the stars.
Yanked between vertical sheets of rock,
twisting higher and higher
sleepers rattle onto a trestle
where dizzying glances down
the river is snaking through granite and shale.
Awakened, we are so small,
what if this rattling dream plunges off?

Cling to the long shadow
curving ahead after its own golden beam,
not to its chimera sliding below us
separate under black water.

IV

Greying into first light,
at last the berth levels out.
Wheels shudder and spark, slowing.
If I press my forehead against the glass
and peer high beyond the blind
I can see a faint thread
bluing above the uttermost pine

and gliding into view
by the matchbox station
a tiny truck parked up a dirt ribbon.
A small figure is waiting
for two men striding away from the train,
shotgun and fishing rod,
French, English, becoming with Native
human specks warming like last stars
the vast dawn of these Precambrian mountains,
setting me, like a child, to waving
for whatever ancient, enduring
need has united them here.

Sideward, the wheels groan and ride
gently down and down.
Faster and faster,
chitter and *chatter*,
yellow flashes off doubling tracks,
lights up streaks on the dusty glass,
shines leaves green, rock brown
as blue pushes cliffs lower and lower
levelling into summer-long grass,
the sky an azure mirror
backing Campbellton's golden bay
where ridges and deep divides
fade around the widening curve
and Canada's dream rattles on
one more day. . . .

Entente

Alma & Yves welcome you with their names
swinging from little black chains
on a postcard lawn.

> *Bienvenue*
> a pansy-filled swan
> floats at the edge of the walk.
>
> *Come on in*
> wrought iron uncurls
> up white steps to the porch.
>
> *Ça va bien?*
> geraniums nod
> over a red window box.

A breeze rushes in off the bay.
Waving by hedges, it skips
over the gravelled drive.

> *Spin-ninn*, the wooden geese whirl.
> *Hee, hee,* an iron squirrel squeaks.
> Three painted skunks won't budge.
>
> *Au revoir* . . .
> Gone down the block,
> you still hear the pansy-filled swan.

But now a marmalade cat
brushing your knee, meows.
—*Did Alma & Yves say goodbye?*

Only the wind hears them whisper
behind the pane's potted fern
and the lace curtains' rustle.

Poetry Class

Wrestle with your angel, I tell them,
and there sits a blond, mustachioed Gabriel
blowing my doom,
talking about *affaires de coeur*
and quoting from Italian.

Every time he glances my way
I feel my old body silken
like the cat lifted before my bath
to slide his thick, black and white fur
across my nakedness.
The cat purred, closed his eyes,
imagining no doubt some giant bird
folding him into her downy breast,
and forgot his usual
clawed bolt to the floor.

As I slide Gabriel through my glance,
in his eyes am I sculpted marble,
my animation *cinéma vérité*?
Does he silently un-stopper my perfume
and calculate how my blush deepens
as I open one more frozen window?
He quotes me into a corner.
Does my breathing scan like his sonnets,
or am I a pink shell where he listens
to Aeolian sheets snap and billow?

Or have daydreams fleshed into life,
fluorescent light a moon,
chalkboard an invitation?
Dare I step across outer space?
Will Gabriel catch me
when I fall?

A Modern Poet and His Muse

I

He wooed her, and wanted her, but she
knocked pedestals across his path,
tottered high and mocked as he
puffed along in rough pursuit,
stumbling over chunks of timeless marble.

Sweeping laurel overhead,
farther out of reach she danced,
page-white skin and silver tresses
flashing recklessness.

She could fly,
gowned in gossamer on sheerest wings,
laughter high and light as rainbows
curving after clouds.
She could sing
mysteries around his heart,
pricking him like nettles slick with honey.

He scanned the countryside:
fields, hills, silent empty green,
no rhythms, rhymes, and images'
ink approximations of her
form and eerie flowing.

He sat down in the dust.
Sad, his fingers drew
circles, moons, stars,
a universe of undulating lines,
primal geometric patterns
waiting to be filled.

Up he jumped.
Enough of antique song!
He'd craft his words
in more familiar tongues.
Feet secure as boulders,
heartbeat sure and strong,
forward he trudged
on free verse of his own.

II

She fluttered round a bend. Waited.
At last, sat down upon a mossy stone.
The vacant landscape bleated.
Again she had no one.
Why? Men pursued her, wooed her,
offered kisses at her airy hem,
wove her daisy chains, or daring,
chased her like old fauns.
Pedestals? But to be hurdled
—better, broken—was the game,
yet, what poet played her way for long?

She kicked a rock aside.
It hurt her feet,
bare and delicate (to suit tradition).
How gritty, dust,
how hard her perch. Such heat
once wings gave way
and crumpled, and she sat
staring at defeat.

Who needed a Muse these days?
No one sang,
at least not to her tune.
Where to scamper once the poets
searched for other means
to spark new lines
and set old syntax free?

Being a shadow only,
she could not
sink into a self that others made.
She was a thousand themes,
ideal that changed
as it found unique shape
in a poet's mind.
Unpossessed: nothing.
Unpursued: unreal.
Yet a potential bound to live
scuffling stony paths,
dragging limpid wings,
weeping at memories
bright with pedestals.

The Artist Passes
In memory of Gilda Mekler

What draws an artist's eye beyond?
Was it an instant's boreal light
revealing darkness
as no more than a veil
between this world and hereafter?

So many thousand times brighter
than earthly watercolours,
did prisms wash
through flesh and bone
onto her mortal paper,
and awed by its brush
she let night's radiant unknown
sweep her higher, higher?

Left behind,
words unread met silence.
Where could she be,
the desktop black,
paintbox shut,
and no footfall?

Many since have felt her breath
between their own vowels and consonants
and trace in vibrant hue and shape
her body still

pointing: an artist is not lost
but smiles along her lilting lines,
a mother, in her children,
a wife within the lingering
embraces of her spouse

for those who create and guide
are never gone
but in their art and love
live on.

Latin Dancer

For Pollyanna

The music muscles crave is like no other,
tugging her to dance, from inside out.
Sultry rhythms quiver, and a samba
swivels satin heels beyond the crowd.

Opened to the tempo's urging,
she becomes the brio motion sings:
shoulders, hips are verbs, each gesture teases
with a smile, a wink, a tossed-off kiss.

Whirling free, her body slips dimension.
Time and space dissolve against wet skin.
Grace embraces strength, and glimpsed perfection
pushes her to sway and spin again.

Sculptor*
For Anne Lazare-Mirvish, 1919-2013

I do it with love.
Fingers thickened with clay
trace his sinewy hands
—*so beautiful*—
spreading into rest.

Posed in her studio,
this aged personage she sculpts
is unfestooned with medals and ribbons,
simply a kind, good man
months widowed
and jagged with grief.
His high cheeks, muscled
by decades of dignified smiles,
bunch much thinner now.
She'll pare some fullness
from his earlier sitting
—but sparingly, for art must be
not a bronzed surface
but the resonance.

She sculpts.
His shoulders sink,
and as the long-pooled darkness
spills across his words,
she halts her scalpel and snaps,
So what? So what?
Loneliness, she knows,
can thicken drop by drop
and choke the spirit down,
an oil-soaked clump of feathers.

He nods, half smiles. She probes.
So hard she yearns to mould
around this wired emptiness
not the once-sleek figurehead
but a fragile ruggedness
that breathes.

Going on, she scolds,
takes little day-by-day braveries.
Yet even as her fingers
pinch and press raw clay,
the wires' layered emptiness
gapes back

—*If you have the art* . . .
she hears her own darkness
swooping in to hover,
doubts spilling over . . .

—*So what? So what?* he snaps,
and she discovers
her subject probes
and shapes the sculptor too.

* *Inspired by Anne's personal account of creating a bust of the late Lincoln Alexander, former Lieutenant Governor of Ontario, not long after his first wife had passed away.*

Pelican

Who knows any bird's true feather?
Plump as a teapot on webbed feet
a pelican wades to her colony
fanning out in a line
to steer small schools of fish into shallows.
One she scoops with her large flat bill.
A second, flips high into air
freeing graceful fins to circle
down and down
into her deep elastic gullet,
a ritual swallowing
more than a million years.

In ancient Egypt, a pelican
embodied the afterlife,
her long neck likened to the shaft
leading to a pharaoh's tomb,
while swooping across great heights
her black-fringed wings,
three metres wide,
awed priests for her power to prophesy
safe passage to the Underworld
after royalty passed on.

Down Under, Aborigines named her Muda,
who during the Dreamtime of creation
pierced by spears,
down Bildimini Hill
let her flowing blood soak Earth
and harden into rainbowed opal.
Scratched, its shimmering tints flared sparks
through grasslands to the Wangkumara,
first tribe to use her gift of fire.

In Mediaeval legend, sadder,
she pecked her breast's white softness
to nourish chicks with her own blood
—wounds too deep to cauterize with physic—
self-sacrifice cathedrals stained in glass
to symbolize a human Christ.

Alas, folklore gave way to science
when a fourteenth-century dentist
Monsieur Guy de Chauliac
needed to clamp down on panic
inflaming so many patients' gums.
Rolling his shirtsleeves up for work,
he mused how his new-fashioned pliers
were shaped like a long, powerful beak
and christened them: pelican.

Jinn

Over here.

High on a shop shelf strewn with old figurines,
side by side, two little white rabbits
whispered to me, *Pick us.*
And even though formed from roughened plaster,
each rounded body, grounded on big paws
curled comfortably into my palm.

How soothing to slide my thumb
around plumped cheeks
and under
long curved ears,
one pair tilted, as if to listen,
the other flopped back, cavalier.
Four small pink eyes bored into mine,
as if both crinkled noses had scented
a succulent lettuce leaf.

And so I carried them home.
to crouch on the table and watch,
still and silent, where I write and read.

Last night,
across the window's full moon
one leapt toward me in a dream.
Tall as my knee,
with glistening fur,
it hopped at my heels from room to room.
Eyes, pink crystals, up it stared
as if to be held and spoken to.
Snuggling into my arms,
its now-silk whiteness stroked me calm.
All the while, its eyes kept burrowing
deeper. I couldn't get free.

In sunlight, on my writing table,
still the plaster pair study me:
Do it. Is that what they say?
Rabbits are symbols of fertility.
—Not only in flesh,
but also in words?

PART 2
Beyond Knowing

Creator

Like so many, one day waking
to ourselves—*alive*—
I ponder Who and Why
undreamed us here,
grounded earth, the stars,
breathed open space, at once
so microscopic, so immense
no eye, no brain can fathom.

Who? Or is it only
what longing cannot bear:
an infinite complexity
spiralling through eons
its soulless imperfection.

Where is the radiant figure
I crave, to comprehend,
to shiver to accept
the brutal amid beauty,
love in spite of evil
—my uneasy wonder?

Looking

In simple things
do we touch God
—earth aromatic after rain,
crickets' dripping chorus,
or light like a clean sheet
the sky pulls taut?

But what of an anthill's scurries from rising water,
that vast impersonal cycle of dawning and darkness
hooking us onto moon's wax and wane?
Against the slow flaming explosions of space
that birth and annihilate stars
does suffering mean nothing?

What else can we do?
Listen to weeds?
Sniff a path among stars?
Feel cold imperfection
in a drop?

Far North

Far north,
when blue curves closer
as if to cup the earth

between outcrop
and pines' needled spaces
mind can almost touch a Presence

until past dusk
the darkness crystallizes
—one after one such stars!

A sprinkle, scatterings, multitudes
layering thicker and thicker
than any imagined vision

glittering from immensities of black,
beyond and beyond
and beyond

—how can a single Spirit
watch over it all?

Who Would Be a God?

"Oh, I would be a god"—Lenny Everson

Who would be a God?—Such juggling!
Scheduling rivers to run backwards
or a crack to lengthen and widen
boiling up black smokers beneath the sea.
And what to do about *Popo* Chang's petunias
soccer-balled by red-necked boys,
or Antarctica melting,
while ants wobble a giant breadcrumb
toward their hungry mountain of sand?
The bluest skies have ignited with suicide drones.
Within the next sixty seconds,
how many thousand more
babies—which genes? what gender?—should be conceived?
Churches, synagogues, mosques, gutters, or temples,
the centuries' dizzying Babel deafens.

Infinities of invisible sprockets!
From orbits to neutrons, keep all spinning
across string theory's ten dimensions.
What of that fat firecracker, chaos?
Forever its sizzle is so tempting
to shatter every well-oiled cam and pinion
in any present and possible universe.

Isn't mere mortal fussing enough of a headache
—to dig from clean laundry two navy socks that match
and remember not to sprinkle the cactus
except every fifteenth day,
let alone halt wars, seed famines,
and recharge a global economy?
Each body is, after all, a whole cosmos
revolving joints in their sockets,
dodging those rogue asteroids
cancer, Parkinson's, pneumonia,
not to mention woofing and warping
around space-time's white hole,
the soul.

Too much!
God only knows.

In Search of New Credos
A glose

Which of the daringly devised creations
can beat us in our fiery enterprise?
We stand and strain against our limitations
and wrest in things we cannot recognize.
—Rainer Maria Rilke

In Mediaeval times a Chain of Being
linked lowly stone to lamb to man to angel.
Even a hungering aphid dared to nibble
the innermost pink of the sacred rose.
Now, from stained glass, wings and paws scatter.
Unfettered too, we tremble. Destinations?
Unknown. No looking back. The wind swallows
our voices. Naked of faith, we muddle onward
snatching at shadows for transfigurations
—but which of the daringly devised creations?

Serve others? Worship Art? Or bend to learn?
Dizzying with choices, back we fall.
Hissing from the grass, a green shadow
coils, hypnotic golden eyes aglow:
Each be your own god. Then heaven's nearer.
Stars? The bushes blink with fireflies.
Moon? Right here—it shimmers in a puddle.
Ripple your vast cosmos with a thumb.
We nod. When we are gods, whose truth or lies
can beat us in our fiery enterprise?

Fiery? Staring at a dandelion
we christen it a newborn sun—as if
a name becomes the thing, breathes life from sound.
But when myriad yellow weeds tuft up
hither and thither, where is east? How spark
dawn from dark without light's fluctuations?
Can petals glow a buried seed to life?
So much for worm's eye views. Look high. At noon
blue burns us with its ancient revelations:
we stand and strain against our limitations.

What's left for us, long since the Chain was broken
rusting over centuries, lost rings
glimpsed in candlelight or chanting vestments?
Far from Europe's spires, one Great Plain
links rock to sweetgrass, wasp to buffalo, to Brave
who, on Raven's wing, strokes wilder skies.
God hunts and fishes this New World. His line
hooks and flashes up that ancient Chain,
while we still shield our gaze, too civilized,
and wrest in things we cannot recognize.

At Midnight

Across the dark lake
silver ripples.
The moon
unbinds her braids.

The Listeners*

Waking in northern darkness,
we grope from tree to tree.
Above, the branches are woven so thick
no stars wink through—we only remember
a black dome over loon-shivered water
netted with lights so clear
they would have lit our way
along this rotting surveyors' swath
iridescent with lichen on long-downed trunks
where feet sink into mould and moss.

What else, beside us,
creeps among trees unseen?
We strain at every snap and rustle
until as shadows shift and thin,
from a distant greying branch
a faint *chirp*,
a *chickadee-dee*
and in answer
chirrups and *cheeping*.

As birches redden,
high in glistening cedar and pine
more and more tiny throats swell the throbbing
with joyous vibrations to welcome dawn
until we, too, like aspen are shivering
that each day—with or without us—goes on
this ancient celebration: returning the light.

* *Read by Lea Harper during her Haliburton Trails and Tours walk, October 16, 2004*

Lake Sounds

Across the misted smoothness of the lake,
thump, a distant paddle drops to ribs
as morning slips to shore.

Hollowed, the air refills with birds'
tchuh-tchuh, too-oo-ee
and *ffflt*

while pines
raise green silences
moist with earlier rain.

Far off,
stilled to satin
wide grey waters wait:

a citied heart has steadied,
gliding in a red canoe
to listen at the centre.

First Snow

First snow
lovely snow

lacing over limp marigolds
and browned grass

lay down cool calm
across our restless dreams

you are a blessing upon
rusted stalks and stems

your graceful flecks of white
make faith seem possible.

(In)Substantial

Millennia ago,
Precambrian,
it was fire.
Now skin scrapes
against rough mass:
northern igneous rock.

Beneath evergreen and aspen,
deeper and deeper
its dark rigidity
haunts the dreams of physicists
as particles, waves,
electromagnetism.

The paradox: ethereal substance.
Matter and shape—illusion.
Science, or mysticism?
At once,
each nano element
flickers *here / not here.*

So could
the black hole of death
reverse if God blinked?

Photon

Inside an atom, a photon whirls
—electromagnetic energy.

Yet, on slowing in its spin,
by freezing to an instant packet of light
it mimics matter
and glints with mass

only to quicken and thaw back
like a neon sign flashing
wave into *particle*:
wave / *particle* / *wave* ...

How solid can our big world be
flickering in quantum space?

God Particle

I do not believe in the Higgs Boson,
a subatomic "God particle"
scientists hope would explain
how energy in the universe
blossoms into mass.

At CERN*, to find it,
deep underground
high energy protons are whizzing around
a 27 kilometre track.

And when they smash?
A "background fluctuation",
"a modest excess of events"
—could that shadow be dark matter?
 "We have not found it yet."

I do not believe in the Higgs Boson,
a "cosmic molasses"
where electromagnetic waves
transform into particles
as they wade and fatten.

—After all,
what makes the molasses?

I believe in the ancient sages'
music of the heavenly spheres
concentrating to a solid
in an immeasurable
slowing of motion.

*European Organization for Nuclear Research,
 Large Hadron Collider, Geneva, Switzerland*

Scientist

A boy cracks open a speckled blue egg.
Inside, he puzzles,
what shapes the robin?

He pries the back
from an old-fashioned clock.
A spring uncurls wheels into motion.

So how can a battery thin as a button
or a watch sliver of quartz
flick out digital seconds?

What is it that shocks
such tiny vibrations?
—or his own heart's tick-tocking?

Spinning Top

A spinning top
bemuses with its blur
until it slows and swivels to one side
where fingers catch
at last its smooth cone
but not its fleeting shimmer.

So twist the wrist
to spin again, again,
and watch, to grasp the moment
solid thins to air,
here / not here
—but where?

Why we stare
when the Dervish whirls
as if divinely mesmerized,
head tilted back,
one palm facing sky,
the other pointed to the ground,

his flaring hem an outward sign
for spirit opening and rising
moonlike to a higher plane,
his ecstasy
the particle becoming
pure energy, a nanophysical wave.

Quest

Try to pin it down
and farther it slips from intellect's fingers.
Quicker—swerve to catch a flash
in the corner of our eye.

Could it be a long awaited
spark from the centre?
Or a mirror within a mirror, within a mirror . . .
diminishing a speck of light?

We build glass houses to survive
the arctic blankness round unknowing,
projecting on transparent walls
what—we must believe—
are more than rainbows.

Balance Sheet Dream

Working the brain's curve
luminous numbers like minuscule beads
interconnect on invisible wires.
Pairings and groupings form harmonies,
sets on the left, with those on the right or beneath.

Ping a black bead, and a red one vibrates,
matching the distance, minus or plus.
Magic, each column shivers, lights up.
Decimals rise and fall.

Winking these long winding caves,
nothing functions alone.
Indissolubles, *have* and *owe*,
1 or 0, and 0 or 1
blink back and forth
each to the other
to balance the binary bond.

Within such minute computations
what starred universe unfolds?

PART 3
Passing Seventy

Secret
For Ezra Schabas

That quiet half-smile, a nod,
what is it the silver-haired know,
graceful in their wrinkles,
edges and angles ground away by time?

Although their breathing slows,
catch the spark from their eyes?
There is more, it hisses,
as if little by little
we too shall understand

the gentling strength of steel
long weathered, well tempered,
how waiting to be struck
yet one more day waking
rings sweet.

Bed

When I was young
I wanted a firm bed
to hold my long body straight
and keep me from nesting
within a sleep too deep
to spring up
with other birds of first light.

Now that I am old
a softer mattress
embraces me
as dream after dream cascades
and the scent of fresh laundered sheets
rises within a nestle of blankets and afghans.

I am in no hurry
to scatter birds.
I savour—I cling to—
their song.

Mini Stroke

Waking?
Or skittered off
a nether slope of the brain?
Fractured into the room-full mirror
daylight is hanging askew,
silences ricochet

and drifting along the hall,
something forgotten
(how many seconds ago?)
didn't happen
—but moments after
remembered—it did
beside the bed
as myself, at the moment
am not (or am I?)
in this overturned world.

Between headache and numbness
notion puffs after notion
across a glare like snow
and rebound into
Who's talking aloud?
and *Whatever happened
on the ceiling?*
as angles slide, spinning and falling
into my aching eyes.

Will gobbling aspirin
thin a clot out of the brain?
Will bright-bright sun straighten
crazy quilting into red stripes
and knock me back into sleep
or point the compass needle north
across a crinkled map of the day
out of this jellybean meantime?

Stressed

It isn't a whale
gulping you whole into its darkness,
but each precise piranha
ripping its toothful of flesh from your bones
that reddens the current
and shocks you upright at 3:00 a.m.
in a bed a-shiver with nerves.

It isn't the shrapnel of worry
or disappointments or fright
razoring into your chest,
but the force field of day after day
magnetizing their mini-weights
until they *thonk* together and strike
—that massive wrecking ball:
a stroke, a breakdown, a heart attack.

It isn't the first, or the only
—why among thousands in the mirror's
rear-view, one particular blur
happens to hurtle you into the smash-up.
It is—remember?—that tiny bug you brushed off
that creeps out from the shadows and bristles
the giant-millipede nightmare.

As the Days Grow Shorter

Bending lower, I fondle
chipped bowls and stained spoons.

Contentment is imperfect,
truth a cracked glass.

But open a cupboard. Out tumble
yellowing memories.

If order unfolds from chaos,
couldn't I also believe

a little silver polish
will rub the ache from dulled days?

—Better than clinging to sticky rings
for fear of being erased.

Tightrope
Threescore and ten

Feet firm
on far-off ground
our middle-aged children gape
up, as yet another of us
is wobbling out crooked
over time's dizzying spaces.

Cockeyed—look, no hands!—
bold stripes and polka dots
deny our silver hair.
We teeter after a dream:
to be wise in a wizard hat,
wit flashing with jester bells,
and acrobatic enough to prance
after whatever airy notions
puff past.

In truth, we are simply
forgiving, not grinning
at our tousled, lopsided lot.
Whether anyone cares or not,
blinking, we totter on,
our tightrope frayed,
but reaching
—how soon?—
over the rainbow.

Eye Surgeon

Wherever I look,
he is there:
in twigs
on distant trees,
in pen-fine outlines
defining my chrome taps,
in a pill bottle's tiny print.
Even stone tiles on the floor
are etched with his intricate landscapes.

When I raise a crystal vase,
snared amid green whorls
a tiny drop shivers
on a rose petal
and I remember his voice
above a blurred watery light,
easing a sting, a pressure,
measured, reassuring
Be calm, all is well.

Turning a page
I read through eyes
no longer only my own,
images made radiant by his hands,
also implanted in my brain:
lenses of his perfect
artistry and caring.

Tiny Bug in the Bathtub

Once, I might have
pinched it in a snatched tissue
and flushed away to oblivion
this speck fleeing across white,
a trapped intruder, offence
against my glistening porcelain.

Wise Persian weavers knew
what I have had to learn:
perfection is God's alone
as each carpet they designed
honoured with one flaw.

Humbled before this frantic life,
instead of death
instant, or exhausted
from slipping up and down
steep white walls,
on a tissue corner
I raise my guest over the rim
to the shared floor of freedom.

Rusting
For my husband

We are rusting,
but on rising,
the rush of water over skin,
first golden glint of juice in a glass
and the brightening rhythms of the day
—*good morning, good morning*
from walls, windows, sunlight—
coax us onward,
step after step slower,
still, in gratitude,
a step.

But how will the day begin
when one of us is gone
to pieces
that hang unworn
in an unopened closet?

Will salt tears moisten wrinkles,
whisky tint the glass
and too many walls
lean silent as windows
shuttering in the dark?

Weighing Ends
For J.W.

Smash out,
rather than suffer
a slow terminal round?

Wouldn't you miss
a lingering backward glance,
rare moments to right
harsh words, a gesture, to bless
glistening memories into place

despite—eyes open—regret
what blossoms and bustles by,
leaving you out, while still in,
conscious: all you loved and touched
is being stripped away

till staying alive narrows
to only your swelling body,
mind and senses tatter,
and final weeks flash into
the steely high voltage of pain.

Able to do nothing
but hang on to that last
atom as long as you can,
the next gasp mattering
less and less,

may you glimpse infinity's *more*
as peace cracks you wide
open into its light.

Finale

Deepening toward indigo
night settles over the garden.
Traceries of leaves and branches
thicken into shadow.

Faint rustle.
Twitters fade.
Held breath.
—Stillness.

Is that how the last
moment will feel:
a distant tiny light,
awaited star?

Passing

Cradling your head on my palm,
as I watch, the tension
filling your veins
solidifies, softens
and you fade
—eyes wide, hardening
to blue shields of light—
into a perfect stillness.

Where is the shiver of spirit
into some purer air?
No wisp? No flash?
—Nothing we speak of
in the dimension of "out there".
Rather, as if
in three slow-motion seconds
whatever sparked this remnant body, spins
inward down through cell, gene, DNA,
to quark.

In the same way, an overblown stamen
shrivelling among petals and leaves
plummets its energy
back within a microcosmic ocean
whispering, promising
perennial seed.

So we, saying goodbye, from this moment
are not apart, not absent,
but simply unfamiliar
forms of each other.

Crossing

Now as you turn toward the falling light
leaving the path, for leaf dapple

nothing can slow your step, nor halt
your soft dissolve into air

a shiver not quite caught in the eye
—yet there

as if in an atom's whirling spaces
is fullness beyond prayer

and aching after your absence
we touch you everywhere.

Grieving

In darkening days
when pulse slows,
a great shaggy bear
fattened on berries, and cranky,
lumbers to sniff out a cave in the rocks,
the warmth of forgetfulness, deep sleep.

Who would urge it to spring
back into sharp light and wind,
to lick only snowflakes swirling the snout,
to skid along ice
even great claws cannot grip
before time's twist in the belly
hungers for a rebirth?

So some wrap around themselves
a thickening memory,
lie down, inhale minutes passing
fed up with foraging, fighting, or fleeing
and fill their hollow with rest
mindless, simply to be.

Conversion

From room to room, each season
has raised new pictures to my walls.
Filigreed gold, wooden ovals,
burnished silver rectangles
frame five generations,
their black and white serene
scattered amid grandchildren's
primary-coloured doodles,
old prints, small pen and inks,
watercolours, and landscape oils.

As age and love humble,
dusting, once a harried chore,
has become transformed
into a ritual of remembering,
each icon in my secular nave
lit not by a candle, but morning light
and after, stepping back,
reverenced by straightening
all into balanced arrangements
—my domestic sacrament.

Return

Looking beyond the horizon,
surely we are not meant
to vanish
but, even as dust,
may quicken green slopes
or bloom within desert sands.

So why the fuss
to preserve bits of paper,
the sparkle of crystal and gold?
Our children
are our net worth.
Grandchildren own our genes.

At best,
millennia hence
some ardent archaeologist
may dig up fragments of bone
and wonder what a hand built
or an airy skull longed.

The rest may compress
into fossil and stone
or pushed deeper
melt into magma
and a billion years after
bubble up and renew the earth.

Wishes
For my daughter

In my next life
after long intermingling
and being reshaped by the earth,
I would return as an opal,
the delicate fires of the poet
shifting with every dip in the light

and you, who loved sowing
tending, and healing,
green into emerald,
believing akin to the ancients
a genuine crystal may bloom
its own leafy *jardin*.

Neither of us would be diamond.
Deeper than all underground,
under the weight of eons
carbon has simplified,
clearing hue and inclusion
to flash as the strongest of gems.

Transparence

On sunlit grass—a *flash*
plumps into a tiny palmful
whirring feathers—the brightness
a hummingbird.

So is our human body too
in this great swirling
cosmic soup of gluons and quarks
formed from a quirk of light?

And in a billion more Earth years
will our fraction of an instant
never again repeat as us
—just so?

Or is our conscious spark enduring
into some distant eon's moment
within an ozone molecule
or silver boiling a bubble through stone?

What if, in a little spider
scurrying over its glistening web,
a million years into the future
I have glimpsed myself?

Idea

*An idea
in the mind of God,*
three hundred years ago
Bishop Berkeley mused
on us, the universe.*

And now, are we
0 and 1, 1 and 0
to a Divine Programmer?
Or clusters
of vibrating spaces
in a quantum physics?

Or is it
our own dreaming
undreaming we exist?

* *A Treatise Concerning the Principles of Human Knowledge, 1710*

EPILOGUE

The Choice

When I have chosen words to be my light
and darkness too

pacing a narrow walk
arch to arch as shadows billow

and have run my palms along damp stones
to catch whatever spark filters through

when I have found a way alone, my beads
translucent as unknowns

and knelt on steps long hollowed
by uncounted ghosts

and felt a massive door thud shut ahead,
heavy key aflame on the far side

and yet have heard the distant voices singing
silver on icy air

then I am told that giving all to words
is worth the harm

and do not even mind
for underneath *in-vain* and *must-not-do*

is that catch-nail—love—
words hang themselves upon.

About the Author

Susan Ioannou's fiction, articles, and poetry have appeared across Canada. She is the winner of an Okanagan Short Story Award, twice a finalist in the CBC Literary Awards, and the recipient of a Works in Progress and Writers' Reserve grants from the Ontario Arts Council. Some of her poems have been translated into Hindi and Dutch, and others set to music for performance in both Canada and Norway. For many years she was Associate Editor of *Cross-Canada Writers' Quarterly/Magazine* and also led writing workshops for the Toronto Board of Education, Ryerson Literary Society, and the University of Toronto School of Continuing Studies. Currently, she directs the online poetry course *Lessons in Writing the Poem*. She is a longstanding member of The League of Canadian Poets and The Writers' Union of Canada.

Her website is: http://www3.sympatico.ca/susanio/

Previous Titles by Susan Ioannou

Chapbooks

– *Spare Words,* (Pierian Press) 1984
– *Coming Home: An Old Love Story,* (Leaf Press) 2004
– *Who Would Be a God?* with Lenny Everson, (Passion Among the Cacti Press) 2004
– *The Merla Poems,* (Wordwrights Canada) 2006

Poetry

– *Clarity Between Clouds,* (Goose Lane Editions) 1991
– *Where the Light Waits,* (Ekstasis Editions) 1996
– *Looking Through Stone: Poems about the Earth,* (Your Scrivener Press) 2007

Children's Novels

– *A Real Farm Girl,* (Hodgepog Books) 1998
– *The Hidden Valley Mystery,* (Wordwrights Canada) 2010

Fiction

– *Nine to Ninety: Stories across the generations,* (Wordwrights Canada) 2009

Nonfiction

– *A Magical Clockwork: The Art of Writing the Poem,* (Wordwrights Canada) 2000
– *Holding True: Essays on Being a Writer,* (Wordwrights Canada) 2008

www.ingramcontent.com/pod-product-compliance
Lightning Source LLC
LaVergne TN
LVHW090037080526
838202LV00046B/3848